Walking-Class Heroes?

Dublin's Remarkable Street-Personalities, 1955-2015

Pictures
& Text
by
Rory
Campbell
+
Photographs by Gerard Brady

First published in Ireland 2015
by
Killiney Hill Press

ISBN 978-0-9932434-0-0

**Typeset in Happy Serif and Adobe Caslon
Printed by Castle Print, Galway
Design and layout: Paula Nolan**

KILLINEY
HILL PRESS

Dedication

My picture-book is dedicated in tribute to Eleanor (1896-1992), a major friend to three generations of the family since the early 1930s; also to the two elder of her four sons, who were friends, neighbours and contemporaries of my mother: David Stuart (born 1921, died in action – North Africa – November 1942), and Robert Stuart (born 1923, died in action – Northern Italy – September 1944).

Their courage humbles me.

Contents

Contents

Preface

by Hilary Pyle

A wanderer is a man from his birth,
He was born in a ship
On the breast of the river of Time.
- Matthew Arnold

As a child I remember homeless 'Uncle George' with his orange hair plastered back who used to visit us, and I suspsect other friends of my parents, from time to time. Son of an aged Canon in Derry, he laughed and twinkled unceasingly behind his thick lenses – so much so that I was seriously puzzled, and one day crept behind the newspaper he was holding to see if it was true that he smiled all the time. I was shocked and sad to find his face long drawn, his eyes devoid of dancing light.

Rory Campbell doesn't intrude so rudely on the characters that intrigue him. He takes them for what they are, and represents them in the guise in which they have chosen to reveal themselves – his earliest memory being of 'Toffee' of the generous hand and wild eye, as an ogre bending down to a child. Toffee's companions are 'Liam Whizz', 'Mr Fox', 'The Angry Brigade', 'Foulmouth'. Not all of his 'perambulating personages' have names, but they dance, and shout obscenities, gesture, walk balletically, or sit frozen in their innerness. Having the cartoonist's unfailing eye and wise pencil he unites this hidden sanctum together with the engaging outer appearance that catches his attention, but he refuses to exploit the vilnerability and the hurt, and respects the 'forty coats' they have cast around them.

Rory Campbell is more than a visual artist, he brings together Ireland's verbal and visual traditions of satire and cartoon from the Táin to Jonathan Swift and from the Sighle na Gig to Michael Healy, in his exquisitely composed vignettes of Dublin's street people. Both traditions have been passed down in his family. His grandfather, the poet Seosamh MacCathmhaoil (Joseph Campbell), a strong supporter of the national movement, started his career showing paintings at the Gaelic League Oireachtas exhibitions. For years he lived in a cottage in Glencree, County Wicklow, and though the family was originally from the North, since that time it has identified with Wicklow, the landscape of the wanderers J.M. Synge created, whether traditional tinkers or drop-outs from conventional society. Rory Campbell himself has studied the wanderers and travellers of his acquaintance in Dublin since he was a boy, and now over the past few years put down what he has observed in crayon images. He represents them for what they are and because he is fascinated by them, and has no personal opinion about these people whom society would call 'unfortunates'. Besides his undoubted skill, and – what any true artist needs – a deep affection for his subject, the tools he uses include an embracing memory, on which he relies.

With his original imagination and impeccable crayon technique, his flexible line and understanding of space, he can render minor details such as the strap of a shoulder bag or a safety pin exactly but unobtrusively so that they become significant in the overall depiction of these lives confined to a solitude in some ways enforced, sometimes chosen. Like Beckett or Jack Yeats, he treats his wanderers with compassion and humour, wasting no time on criticism or sarcasm, other than in the startled reaction from a passing cat or two, themselves wanderers, bewildered by the rage or antics of a human.

In some ways these characters from Dublin streets – gathered here in a group unbeknownst to themselves – could be counted as lucky because they have accepted the limitations of their separate existences, and journey independently through life as quasi-whole persons (if seemingly eccentric), protected by the permanent masks which they have forged for themselves as shields against society's cruel weapons and unsympathy. It is the beauty of the artist's conceptions – a beauty as old as 'Les Très Riches Heures du Duc de Berry', and as young as Chagall and Giacometti –that persuades us to this debatable thought. As an accomplished illustrator, and a lover of literature, dance and music, Rory Campbell has allowed his modern manner to draw on all centuries and from all of the arts for its idiomatic poetry, and instinctively associates his personages with classic literary prototypes as far back as Anglo-Saxon times who have woven their destined way through the human plight. In his images, benign memory bathes each personality in an even glow. For the length of the turning of a page each basks in the limelight, star of his or her own space, the only shadows adding harmonies to the silent music surrounding them.

He can be quite candid in descriptions of despair, wrath, and hopeless imbecility. However, the beauty of his conception embodies the eternal element of the human spirit in all of his people, and assigns to them an inherited spirituality perpetuated through centuries of image makers before him. Mercifully this holy spirit can still express itself through the working hands of the artists of this materialist world.

Hilary Pyle

KILLINEY OBELISK AND BAY IN THE LATER 19TH CENTURY, *by Patrick Duffy.*

This view was little changed even in the late 1950s and mid–1960s, as book and postcard photographs show. Indeed, the card's reverse reads: "This majestic bay, often referred to as 'the Bay of Naples in Ireland', is only a few miles from Dublin. It is without question one of the splendours of Ireland."

Introduction

by Rory Campbell

My early childhood in mid-1950s Ireland seemed very peaceable. Our home, ten miles south of Dublin, was a backwater partly sheltered by magnificent rookery-crowned beech trees, with good farmland on all sides, Killiney beach very near, and Wicklow's foothills just inland.

The summer of 1955 was unusually warm and sunny, with record temperatures, and is partly remembered for the fact that poet Patrick Kavanagh, post-surgery, spent many daylight hours lying on the grassy bank of the Grand Canal near Baggot Street bridge without jacket, shoes or socks, feeling reborn – which he celebrated in two sonnets.

Among my very earliest memories are the visits of a ragged old down-and-out, who'd arrive at our front door in need of money, clothes or food. An older friend of my father since the 1930s, he had mysteriously gone off the rails, and was living rough in a ruin or hovel two miles away, towards Enniskerry. He was respectful and friendly, always bringing toffees for me and my elder brothers, hence the nickname we gave him: 'Toffee'.

So, from my first consciousness of a wider world, tramps were deemed a recognised sector of society. On one of our 78 rpm records by Delia Murphy, which begins "I'm a rambler...". She sang –

"I'm a long way from home,
and if you don't like me,
well, leave me alone!"

Around this time 'Waiting for Godot' – whose author Samuel Beckett had grown up two or three miles away – was receiving international acclaim. Its principal *dramatis personae* were in the tradition of Charlie Chaplin's tramp character, and of Laurel and Hardy in their classic comedies which the new medium of film had brought to the world.

The 1950s also saw the emergence of a superior and influential comic-paper for Britain and Ireland, *The Eagle*, which my eldest brother got each week. I marvelled at Frank Hampson's stunning artwork in his thrilling 'Dan Dare' strip-cartoon adventures, with their rich colouring and dramatic lighting effects – and still do. But in the *Eagle* Annuals, Dare's heroism was complemented by a humorous 'Waldorf and Cecil' cartoon story, about a genial tattered hobo and his boy companion who journeyed together, above reproach, and noble-spirited. During the 1960s *The Eagle* declined, but I was now noticing in

To best depict these street personalities, an academic, painterly method (as here demonstrated, for instance, in Max Beerbohm's impression of brilliant Society Portraitist John Singer Sargent) in NOT recommended.

Hergé's *Tintin* books that their Belgian creator, Georges Rémi, rarely failed to introduce vagrants, eccentrics and madmen, some disturbingly true-to-life.

Of course this focus is nothing new in great culture. Artists and writers have always included conspicuous 'Outsiders' in their oeuvre: in paintings by Breughel, Goya and Géricault for instance; in literature like *King Lear* where Edgar disguises himself as crazy beggar Tom O'Bedlam, or in Tolstoy's *War and Peace*, when as Napoleon is advancing on Moscow, a self-appointed prophet declaims to the city's fairly inept Governor General, Count Rostopchin, or the 'Trampers' who threaten gentle-folk in Jane Austen's *Emma*, not to mention myriad larger-than-life or extraordinary characters encountered in other books.

As a teenager venturing into Dublin more often, myself and friends were mildly intrigued by unusual personalities we espied, and who seemed part of the 1960s' vivid diversity, some sharing common characteristics: spending most of the day walking through crowds and streets intently and alone, rarely talking to other people or making eye contact, perhaps carrying their belongings in bulging plastic bags, yet undeniably sustained by basic physical strength, vigour, and even vitality, though their exposed and mobile lifestyles would take a gradual toll on their health. Living on the margins, the bleak periphery, is unremittingly precarious, trying to survive a bit longer, on the edge of a terrible yet indifferent abyss just beyond.

In general, their single-minded pattern of behaviour rarely altered (though it sometimes deteriorated), nor did their facial expressions: they each had one persona. I got the impression that they didn't waste time talking to fellow humans because they had learned over the years from bitter experience that it was not worthwhile. (Jesus at his trial knew there was no point in trying to reason with or explain to his inquisitor, and fell silent, no doubt infuriating some opponents. Earlier, he had asserted that the 'poor will always be with us', and I would imagine that, likewise, these noticeable, marginalised and socially-excluded street denizens also will always be with us, especially in towns and cities.) Dublin has long had its A-Z of 'Characters', from natives 'Bang Bang' to 'Zozimus', probably more than in capital cities abroad, thanks to a well-tested street-treadability, but especially to Ireland's traditional poverty, pressures and privations. Mad-Ireland couldn't hurt everyone into poetry!

And there are exotic blow-ins from overseas, a dramatic example of whom was the French dramatist and opium addict Antonin Artaud. Involved in the 'Theatre of Cruelty' at home, he came to Ireland in 1937. Claiming his walking stick was the magic staff of Saint Patrick and previously of Jesus, he was apprehended by Gardaí in Milltown, jailed in Mountjoy for six days, then deported back to France as an "undesirable and destitute alien".

Among reasons for embarking on these studies was that I needed to challenge any ability I might have with an extended series of cartoon-like portraits, and to test my memory for details last glimpsed 30 or 50 years ago. I was also challenged by those specific memories as 'moving targets', blurry images in my mind evanescent as the changing light on a scene when Claude Monet was endeavouring – at lightening speed – to capture with oil-paint on canvas one particular moment of a day. I didn't refer to photographs, nor do I recall more than a couple that could be availed of. I also wanted, as always, to consider 'memory' per se. Happily, viewers of the work-in-progress immediately recognised specific individuals.

At the same time, I was reacting against the increasing bombardment from the mass-media of photos and caricatures of celebrities, many of whom I know nothing about, who seem addicted to seeing themselves grinning on front pages of tabloids and magazines in order to feel they exist.

We are used to picture books about a city, its history, architecture and its memorable inhabitants through the ages; but the unconventional street personalities who are in evidence for a period, even decades, are integral fixtures of the street scape too – for a while. Whenever one of them disappears for good, it is not noticed immediately. A few citizens will remember him or her, but eventually those memories will fade and vanish. If there were any snapshots, there's a risk they might be of an untypical or wary posture. Gerard Manley Hopkins recommended unobtrusive awareness in an observer,

"…where a glance
Master more may than gaze, gaze out of countenance."

By summoning back from the shadowy edges of my mind, and even from the grave, a representative selection from more than 60 years of Dublin life, and recreating them on a 2-D page, I am (literally) drawing attention to some tough folk who have very rarely been portrayed as a distinct sector or class of a Nation's population, excepting Scotland for instance, where a slim volume was published in 1857, *Glasgow Characters*, written by journalist Peter Mackenzie. He re-used small black-and-white caricatures, engravings and silhouettes by earlier illustrators of quaint figures like 'Hawkie' (on crutches, with a battered stove-pipe hat), Blind Alick, Feea The Poor Idiot Boy, Raby Nation, flageolet-playing Wee Willie White, Baulty Payne, 'Hirstling' Kate, and others. Raconteur Mackenzie admits that his text is "rambling", like the citizens he describes!

Having endeavoured to include all who seem to demand a portrait, over time I have become almost possessive of "My Lost Sheep"!

Since beginning, I've been asked quite frequently, "Will you include such-and-such a person one used to see?" At this point I sometimes have to answer that self-publicists, 'Professional eccentrics' and bores are excluded: they are not the real thing, the utterly unanticipated, raw actuality.

All the same, I regret that some characters were before my time, or in a rarely visited suburb: like Johnny Forty-coats, who wore layers of ragged clothing, with tin pans dangling from his person; Hairy Lemon, whose face lived up to this moniker; or the Sandymount/ Irishtown picarooney wheeling his rattling, tyreless bike heavily laden with recently scavenged scrap (John Behan would have the ability to capture his essence in a bronze sculpture); or even some bag lady in Balgaddy. Yet I never intended my project to end up as a mere 'Tramp-spotting: the complete Guide for Dublin'.

GLASGOW CHARACTERS.

HAWKIE.

CAPTAIN PATON.

THE REVEREND JOHN AITKEN.

MAJOR

HIRSTLING KATE.

Beards recur through these portraits (though to my relief, a quarter of the 'sitters' are women), but in the Dublin of the 1950s and early '60s, unlike elsewhere in the Western World, beards were not uncommon, especially among the artistic and cultured community. During their early years, before the wider success of 'Seven Drunken Nights', the five member of the band, the Dubliners, were informally dressed, non-shaving bohemians, unconcerned about conformity, disapproved of by the genteel. (Similarly, a last refuge of the Teddy-boy in mid-1960s Europe, – years before the Rock'n'Roll Revival, was Bray, North County Wicklow, "The Last Resort", where Sharkey, a local 'ted', his cow-lick quiff greasily hideous, smashed up 'The Lido' cayfe's juke-box with a chair, in a typical spasm of rage). – These anecdotes of styles outmoded abroad give some context of Ireland as quite cut off from the contemporary modern world, insular. But only quite: after finishing, I saw that representatives of various races had cunningly crept into the scenario.

While showing emerging pictures to a handful of friends and fellow artists, most asked for information about the actual people portrayed. Consequently, each image is accompanied by explanatory text, as brief as possible. At times, a line or lines from literature are more appropriate than my own words, reminding me that the university student narrator in Flann O'Brien's *At Swim Two Birds* suggested that an author could shamelessly lift whole chunks out of other writer's books; could 'sample' suitable descriptions of emotions, states of mind, etcetera, rather than bother to describe them afresh. (He made no mention of copyright law!). G.M. Hopkins, who felt himself an outsider, who felt the ache or agony of exclusion, especially during his final years which were in Dublin, wrote:

"I am gall, I am heartburn. God's most deep decree
Bitter would have me taste: my taste was me;
Bones built in me, flesh filled, blood brimmed the curse.
Self-yeast of spirit a dull dough sours. I see
The lost are like this, and their scourge to be
As I am mine, their sweating selves; but worse."

About 1000 years earlier, anonymous Old-English poem 'The Wanderer' contains an ultimate acceptance of 'Wandering':
"Wyrd bið ful aræd"
("Fate is truly inexorable"!)

Rory Campbell, 2014

"Ce monstre…
mon semblable,
mon frère!"
– Charles Baudelaire, 1857

"I got to keep movin', I got to keep movin',
… Hell-hound on my trail,
Hell-hound on my trail, hell-hound on my trail."
– Robert Johnson, 1937

"Certain habitués of the streets are worth recording."'
– Reverend Canon F.F. Carmichael:
'Dublin – A Lecture', 1907

Prequel:

A trio slightly before my time (– A Threequel?)

'Once upon a time in… Westmoreland Street?'
(– *Study towards an image of 'Bang-bang*).

Dear old – Rare oul' – 'Bang-bang', a lovely – a daarlin' man – by all accounts.

BORN in 1906, for decades Thomas Dudley (influenced by many Westerns he'd watched since childhood) roamed city-centre streets, or perched on the back-step of trams and then buses, occasionally slapping his rump as if it was a horse's, pointing his ancient key and shouting "Bang-bang, you're dead!" many hundreds of times some days, other days less.

Coincidentally, Cher and Sonny Bono's 1966 song 'Bang-bang' would be an apt response from any of his phantom-cowboy victims, as his same exclamation heard thousands of times during a couple of days must have seemed "that awful sound".

In the early 1970s his sight deteriorated, and he retired to the Rosminian home for blind men in Drumcondra. He now insisted on being addressed as 'Lord Dudley', this new persona perhaps influenced by the Viceroy to Ireland of 1902-1905 (immediately prior to his own very humble birth), lavish-spending Lord-Lieutenant, The Earl of Dudley, William Humble.

Surely no-one does 'Folie des grandeurs' or Delusions of Grandeur, better than Irish people in recent years?

'Bang-bang' died peacefully, with his boots off, in 1981. Despite written and spoken anecdotes about him, very few pictures (if any) or photographs exist: there are a handful of snaps from his last years. Ireland too much tended to promote a verbal rather than visual tradition; and still does.

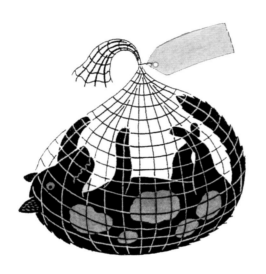

'Hairy Lemon'

(artist's impression)

HIS nick-name probably derived from the shape and complexion of his stubbly head.

During the 1930s and 1940s he tended to good-humouredly saunter around the suburbs of North Dublin like Cabra and Drumcondra, sometimes earning cash by catching unlicensed dogs, stoically enduring the material privations of 'The Emergency' (World War Two) wearing pieces of car-tyre rubber fastened around his feet instead of shoes, then dying soon after 1950.

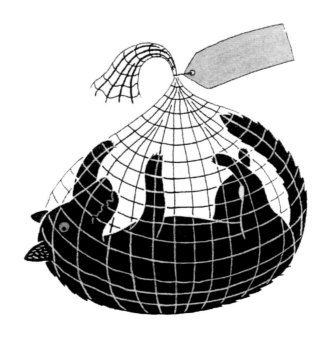

'Johnny Forty-coats'
(P.J. Marlow)
Saint Valentine's Day, 1943

NOT only was he swathed in a plethora of overcoats, but from them dangled (and jangled?) a multitude of tin cans. He preferred to stand at certain vantage-points in the Thomas Street area of The Liberties district, where he would beg. Like 'Bang-bang' he confined himself to just one phrase, repeated over years. His was, '"Give us a penny!" Harry Kernoff depicted him in at least one of his topographical watercolours, circa 1940.

Note photographer's shadow!

'Toffee'

AMONGST my very earliest memories are the visits of a ragged old down-and-out at our front door, in need of food, money or clothes. Friendly and deferential, he always offered toffees to me and my elder brothers.

When my father was studying Chemistry at Trinity College during the early 1930s, 'Toffee' became a friend, visiting his room there and enjoying a glass of poitín that my father was adept at procuring. 'Toffee', not a student, and older, was then working, eventually achieving an eminent position in his field. But by the mid-1950s his world was disintegrating badly; he had increasingly relied on 'pep-pills' (Amphetamines) when their deleterious side-effects were not yet understood, his wife had left him for another man, and he began to live rough for some years.

One time my father gave him a good tweed jacket, no longer needed; but a week or so later 'Toffee' returned, wearing the jacket – now filthy and delapidated.

About fifteen years later, c.1970, at a party, my parents unexpectedly met him again, old now but rehabilitated, spruce and benign. He explained how badly his regular use of 'Speed' had affected his life and career.

In retrospect, I wonder if it was a uniquely Irish combination of pep-pills AND poitín which hastened such dereliction?

'Liam Whizz'

THE speed in this man's life was the frenetic pace of his walking. For years one saw him, marching intently at the same intense pace, as if to some immensely important event.

"For my part, I travel not to go anywhere, but
to go.
I travel for travel's sake."
    - Robert Louis Stevenson.

'Forty-coats'

NOT to be confused with a children's TV character, or with Dublin vagabond 'Johnny Forty-coats'.

Probably there has always been a 'Forty-coats', in every area. Here, he is in summer attire, not the full layerage. He seemed strong as a tank, completely self-contained, and stubborn to boot. Woe betide anyone unwise enough to block his advance: weak as a kitten, such a hapless person would be flipped aside, limply like a rag doll or flimsy wooden skittle.

'A slow Hokey-cokey to … What mysterious music?'

ADVANCING slowly, every third step or so she lifted one leg high, as if to step over a log. Her tangled hair and dog anticipated 'Dennis the Menace' and 'Gnasher' in *The Beano* comic (who eventually usurped the front page from gentle 'Biffo the Bear'). Though a woman of independent means, from a cultured family, who collected her regular allowance from the bank, some nights she chose to sleep in a handy church.

'Mr Fox'

WHO could ignore or forget this pair?

But the animal wasn't happy: when brought to TCD's life-drawing classes, it would slink, cowed and wretched, into a dark corner, and as we sketched the beautiful young, English, nude models, we would occasionally hear an uneasy clinking and slithering of the chain – like in a Dickens tale, or old ghost story.

Its keeper didn't communicate with the rest of us, mostly students – and younger than him. He seemed pale and woebegone, preoccupied and wasted by broodings or resentment.

Usually, a respected artist would attend, and make suggestions if necessary or asked, for instance sculptor John Behan or painter Brian Bourke. The latter, though one of Ireland's best artists since the early 1960s, had his hand nipped by the philistine fox – or claims so! He remembers, as does Behan, its guardian as English, but can also recall a second man with a fox in Dublin. Similarly, Saint Patrick was British, and there were two of HIM!

An old friend from those days remembers alternative clothing: a shabby sheepskin coat, the upper back ripped and lacerated by the creature's claws as it crouched on his shoulders. If I'd been older and wiser, I would have confronted this captor about his treatment and confining of a wild beast, reminding him of William Blake's couplet:
"A robin redbreast in a cage
Puts all Heaven in a rage."

'Moses'

DURING these student years, I arranged a rehearsal space at the same venue as the life-drawing classes for a grateful playwright much older than myself, whose earlier drama had provoked some notoriety at the Royal Court Theatre, London, in the 1960s. I was struck by the suffering of years etched on his face, also the love in his eyes for ungrateful Mankind. I don't know if his new play ever reached the stage, but a couple of years later, with a change of name, he established a small long-term camp on the edge of Sandymount strand, with one or two female acolytes, like some Prophet in the wilderness.

But the Devotee followed at a respectful exact distance: she could not approach any closer.

After some years he bowed out, like Prospero in Shakespeare's *Tempest*:

> *"But this rough magic*
> *I here adjure;*
> *I'll break my staff,*
> *Bury it certain fathoms in the earth,*
> *And deeper than did ever plummet sound,*
> *I'll drown my book."*

The Angry Brigade: Her

STALKING alonog purposefully, rancour seething, muttering imprecations, the hatchet-faced hag …

Perhaps I'm being a little unfair?

(NOTE: Cats hate aggro and noisy disruption; when shouting or violence erupt, they scarper and lie low, discretion being the better part of valour.)

The Angry Brigade: Him

"HOWL, HOWL, HOWL, HOWL."
- Shakespear, *King Lear*

FOR a while, in smarter streets, this man would loudly quarrel with, and scream furiously at, an invisible opponent. I could almost see tiny black devils like whirlygigs water-beetles zig-zagging ceaselessly around him, always avoiding his maddened flailing arms.

Polite society stepped past discreetly, as if unaware of such ear-splittingly overt agony of mind. If, as Thoreau wrote, "The mass of men lead lives of quiet desperation", this fellow's desperation was very noisy indeed!

I wondered: how does a fellow-human help such a tortured victim, how sooth such irrational rage, how heal "this tormented mind tormenting yet" (G.M. Hopkins)? Does one have to wait for the acute affliction to burn out, and then step in to peel him or her off the pavement?

Or can only someone like Jesus actually personally confront such a threatening frenzy as he did with violent lunatic 'Legion' who lived among the Gadarene tombs? We are told that somehow and quickly he got to the heart of the chronic problem ("and now also the axe is laid unto the root"), and suitably dramatically, with two thousand pigs running down a steep slope into the sea of Galilee.

'Food, and for thought'

HE wore the same garb, summer and winter; she wore the same Mod-fashion style well into middle-age, as if trapped in a 1967 time-warp. But what better year to linger in, with its 'Summer of Love' and when everything good seemed fresh or possible?

(In fact, they weren't acquainted).

The Prince of Pain

THOUGH young and glamorous, it seemed his head was wrecked by drugs, or spiralling down some vortex, just as externally, his mongrel-accompllices' leads entwined and tugged him, paralysing any progress along the footpaths.

"O the mind, mind has mountains; cliffs of fall
Frightful, sheer, no-man-fathomed. Hold them cheap
May who ne'er hung there. Nor does long our small
Durance deal with that steep or deep."
- G.M. Hopkins

I could imagine him living – squatting – in some small, damp, semi-derelict gate lodge (nowadays renovated, valuable).

My Concise Oxford Dictionary defines Catalepsy as "Trance or seizure with loss of sensation ... accompanied by rigidity of the body."

Could this young man's situation be more concisely described as 'Dogalepsy'?

Christy

OVER years he increasingly resembled an archetypal 'pathetic clown'; and when members of the public noticed and laughed at him, he became pleased and honoured, playing up to his small audience.

(Similarly at the end of the film 'Zorba the Greek', the Cretan village-simpleton is flattered and mollified by the locals' mockery and innuendo.)

Beggar With Bottle

DESPITE his begging for money, and that alarming sickly-sweet stink of strong liquor off him, he struck me as one of the most intelligent of all these street personalities: like a character of Dostoyevsky.

Grinning cunningly as he thrust out his palm, he had pride enough to despise us do-gooders who gave him coins, us so superficial because we obviously knew nothing of life's dark depths, degradations and complexities.

(When erstwhile friends Ernest Hemingway and F Scott Fitzgerald met for a last time, the latter announced they could no longer communicate with each other – the gulf was now too wide – because Hemingway spoke with the authority of success, whereas he himself spoke with the authority of failure.)

Disillusioned as to the benevolence of human nature and society, this beggar looked down on, or needed to look down on, his bland benefactors.

Noah

I'VE known him, on and off, for much of my life. When a teenager he had already developed an encyclopaedic knowledge of motor sport. At the same time, like countless young people in the mid-1960s he was increasingly fascinated by Afro-American music, Blues and Rhythm'n'blues especially, sending to the USA for unobtainable record-albums unseen in Ireland before. Stark, impassioned, wailing, searing Blues, gritty yet rich in artistry, blasting out of the wireless or mono record-player, had great impact – and still has.

After school, he spent six months in Italy to improve his Italian, based in Perugia but also searching out that country's great art, hitch-hiking around Western Europe to Grand-Prix races and major motor events, and sending back to Ireland superbly vivid, typically funny letters.

Returning home, he dropped out of University after a year, living a wild-and-woolly hobo existance for years, then settling. He is impressively strong, with a detailed memory of his past.

"Now, you probably call him a tramp;
I know it goes … deeper than that:
He's a … *Highway Chyle.*"
- HENDRIX, 1967

Man With Briefcase

I FIRST became aware of him, conversing with himself, oblivious to the external world, as he regularly photocopied accumulations of yellowing newspaper cuttings, which seemed to me random dead stuff from a spiritual desert, a meaningless void.

And yet, I often photocopy articles and images from 'papers and magazines.

Siblings?

SUMMER, Autumn, Winter, Spring, their attire was always thus, ready for all eventualities of weather; they did not speak.

Then, after a couple of years, he only appeared alone – and I inquisitively wanted to approach him to ask "Where is she, your companion who you escorted and protected?"

Trolley Lady & Vagrant

TWO for the price of one, but like the Bibliophiles, this pair were unaquainted.

If representatives of that particular type known as 'French Intellectual', with their assertions about personal freedom, rejection of conformity, a basic meaninglessness or absurdity of existence, 'l'acte gratuit' (motiveless actions), etc, saw this gentleman, I surmise they might acclaim him.

He wandered completely at random – free in a way – his journey unpredictable, one moment lurking in a blocked-up doorway, the next suddenly lurching off the pavement across a street; sometimes by chance treading in the footsteps of playwright Antonin Artaud who, having come from France for six weeks in 1937, claiming that his knotty walking-stick was the legendary staff that previously belonged to Jesus and Saint Patrick (the 'Bachall Isu'), was detained by Gardai in the grounds of Milltown Institute of Theology and Philosophy, and incarcerated in Mountjoy Prison for six days, before being deported home. (A kindly Irishman who conversed with Artaud during his Irish jaunt, immediately realised that the French pilgrim was "travelling light in the upper storey"!)

Perverse Sartre and beady-eyed De Beauvoir might have enjoyed, and congratulated themselves on, hailing the man in my picture as a Saint alongside Jean Genet and Joseph Stalin. But then, they got many things spectacularly, even criminally, wrong.

If Dublin's Jonathan Swift was to re-write 'Gulliver's Travels', he could include among the risible Savants and Boffins that Gulliver encounters at the 'Grand Academy of Lagado' various self-willed Gallic perpetrators of competitively batty theories, despite their fierce advocacy of Human Reason.

The infinitely superior (in my mind) Simone, Simone Weil (1909-1943), an almost exact contemporary of De Beauvoir, both of them Parisians, was one of the thinkers and activists NOT of the above circus; she would have had a profound and penetrating empathy with my 'Walking Class Heroes' for a start – I hope.

Mind you, when she worked for the Free-French in war-time England, General De Gaulle thought <u>her</u> a little crazy!

Simone Weil

Perambulating Personages: 'Bag-City, here we come!'

THIS sweetly apple-cheeked old lady reminded me of my Paternal Grandmother, Nancy. But rather than living in a rustic cottage, where roses and honeysuckle entwined and clustered around the front door, she resignedly and undeviatingly plodded city-centre streets, for some years.

Later, I suddenly noticed that I hadn't seen her for quite a while: such people don't announce their imminent retirement from further street appearances.

('Bag City' was a Bag and Suitcase Emporium in Moore Street).

Foulmouth

'MEN do not know whither the demons go in their wanderings'!
- from *Beowulf*

This merry fellow, this jovial gentleman …

Don't be fooled!

Of all these street-personalities, he was the only one to be <u>heard</u> first: I'd think that a couple of animated conversationalists, still out of sight, were approaching along the pavement, but then … 'Foulmouth' would stride past the window, alone.

He spent each day, year after year, smartly attired, swaggering, rollicking through streets broad and narrow, uttering an endless stream of verbal filth, relishing his obscenities and scatology, his cheeks a bit flushed, his eyes glinting and rolling excitedly, delighted with himself for such daring naughtiness, at his complete freedom: a non-stop, near-eternal 'Tourette's Syndrome'.

In his language, certainly,
       "His roguish madness
Allows itself to anything."
- Shakespeare, *King Lear*

Decades later I was still seeing him, slower, a bit shrunken, but remarkably well-preserved, comfortably wrapped up, muttering more quietly to himself, unrepentant.

"I wandered north, and I wandered south,
By Golden Lane and Patrick's Close,
The Coombe, Smithfield and Stoneybatter,
Back to Napper Tandy's house.
Old age has laid its hand upon me …"
-from the ballad *The Spanish Lady*, by Joseph Campbell

Patriotic Cleansers

HAD he misheard lines in Dylan's song as

> *"Don't follow leaders,*
> *Wash the parking-meters…"?*

It's said he left his native North of Ireland to get away from the post-1967 'Troubles', and suggested doing this job to Dublin Corporation – who created the position for him alone, which he dutifully performed for years, a popular figure.

<u>She</u> had perfect skin, a cat-loving one-person Guardian of the City's spiritual well-being.

Then almost overnight, those familiar parking-meters, design icons, disappeared from pavement edges. When I contacted Dublin Corporation in order to view again their exact dimensions, I was referred from department to department, as futiley as in a tale by Franz Kafka. Officials had forgotten, or 'dis-remembered' them, as if they had never existed.

Sadhu

"OFTEN the solitary man, sad at heart, must tread the paths of exile; Fate is truly inexorable." So spoke the wanderer, mindful of hardships. "I know intruth that it is a wise habit for a person to heed his contemplations."
– from *The Wanderer* (Anglo-Saxon poem)

Drifting mournfully around Dublin over decades, as if pondering 'World-sorrow', – the transience and sorrows of this world – his discouraged mood was in perfect harmony with his look of pathos, of exquisite self-pity, consistently picturesque:

"But I will wear my heart upon my sleeve
For Daws* to peck at."
- Shakespeare, *Othello*

*Jackdaws

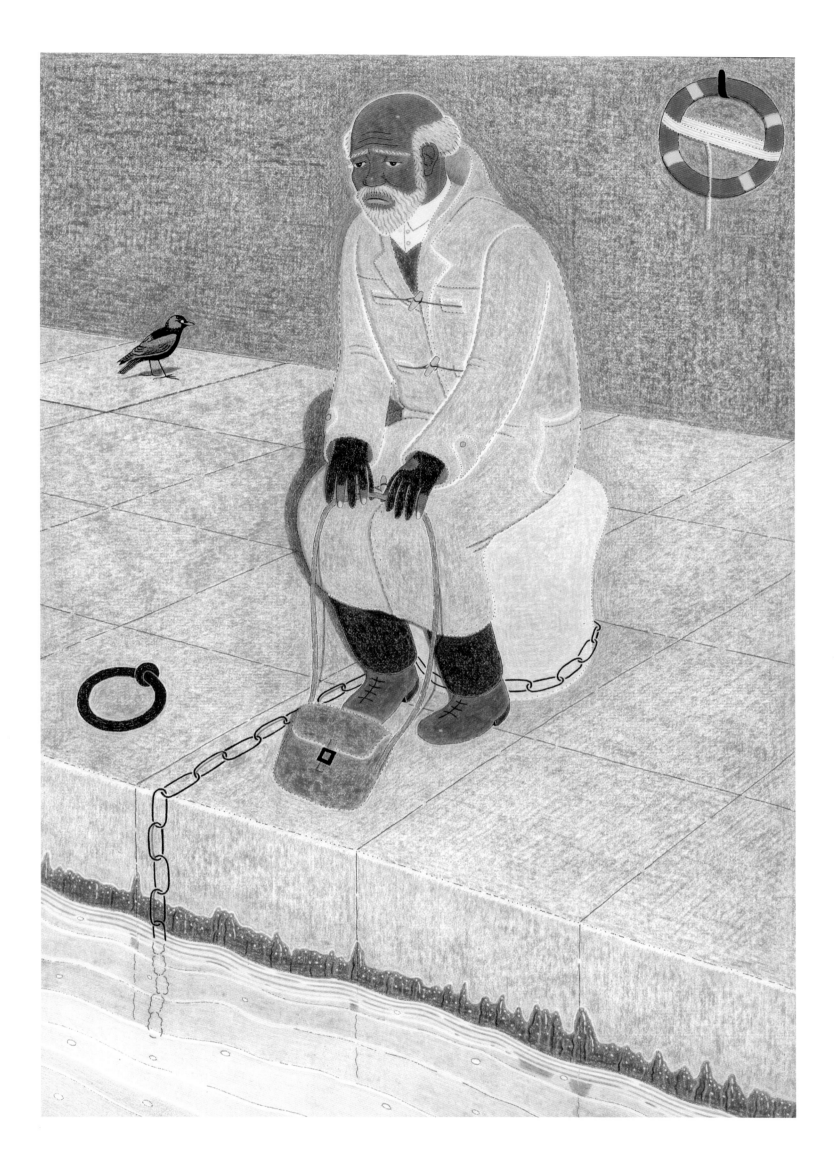

Japanese Man in TCD

ALSO from the mystic Orient, a fixture around Trinity College for decades as if engaged in scholarly research, indignant if a student should sit in the library-seat which he preferred, occasionally yelping suddenly, he aged badly, neglecting to dye his hair, creeping along neighbouring streets as if seized-up or in chronic pain, eventually wasting into emaciation, like a famine-victim.

In late 2007, when food left outside his flat sat uncollected for days, police forced the door and found him dead – of natural causes –at 73. *The Irish Times* also reported that Masahiso Matubara had grown up in Tokyo (contemporaneous with Yoko Ono, incidentally) and studied in Norway and Paris before arriving in Dublin circa 1980. At TCD he wrote a thesis on Islamic journeys for which he received an M.Litt in 1987, but since then he was barred from the library for writing in text books.

Though very deaf, he used sign-language and written notes; and understood at least seven languages – including Irish and Russian.

Uomo Vecchio

"HEY, I'm foreign, ancient and picturesque, likewise. Can I be included with that previous pair?"

Rory: "Well… that sloping alleyway doesn't look like Liffey Street to me. Where exactly are you?"
"A town called Piazza Armerina, near Enna, in the very centre of Sicilia …Sicily."

Rory: "Then I'm afraid you don't quality for this book, Signor; but be thankful you live on a sunny, civilised and cultured island, no doubt free from the shenanigans and corruption so endemic here in rainy Ireland. Buona Fortuna, Signor!"

End of the Sicilian idyll.

A Hero

FOR years – throughout each working day – he manned his specific pitches, performing diligently his rôle, stoically enduring the flow of crowds and changing weathers, respected by – how many?

Then he no longer appeared, and the populace hurried along as always.

Mary Dunne

ALMOST every day, for twenty-five years, dressed impeccably in richly-coloured 1950 modes, carefully made up and coiffed, she danced her personal ballet on the spot where Nelson's Pillar stood.

Twirling, then executing brief trotting forays along the pavement, genuflecting slightly – almost crouching, arms and hands dramatically expressive, fingers twiddling, absorbed in the sequence of movements, she was our very own Ecstatic Dancer: Catholic Ireland's answer to the inspired Sufi or Whirling-Dervish, her vitality sustained by some never-failing Spirit, a long-term, self-choreographed Performance-Artist.

During 2003, as if commensurate with this perennial Celebrant, and as if to mark her quarter-century residency, O'Connell Street was en-spired with a silvery, shimmering, 120 metre perpendicular tapering spike; like her also apsiring into the heavens.

> ... *"(S)he who kisses the Joy as it flies*
> *Lives in Eternity's sunrise."*
> - William Blake

Bibliography: Liam Fay's *Beyond Belief: A Mind-Blowing Pilgrimage Through Religious Ireland*. (Hot Press books, 1999)

Pen-man

THE same morning, the sun is rising over the Irish Sea dazzlingly, and this particular Pillar of Society is about to commute by rail along the coast to Dublin, as he has done for many years.

He is au-fait with current market conditions, bang up-to-date on fluctuations in the Stock Exchange, and fully briefed about the state of the world economy...

Or is he?

Sven Fork-Beard (Viking King) or Sisyphus?

CONDEMNED by Fate to endlessly walk the roads of a wasteland-like Dublin, scorched by the sun in summer, scourged by icy winds in winter, he always bore an immensely heavy pack, surely physically damaging or crippling, eventually?

Florence

FOR decades, robed and heavily cowled in black, with dark eyes gazing out of a narrow slit, like an Arab-woman from a *Tintin* book, she pulled her trolley through the city-centre.

At Anti-Apartheid Annual General Meetings she would seriously interrupt important matters and weighty business concerning the unjust situation in Southern Africa with her unrelated plaints, and I marvelled at the patience and diplomacy of Founder-Officials like Terence McCaughey, Gearoid Kilgallen and Kader Asmal as they tried to humour her into silence. After dealing with her, Asmal must have found his work since 1994 in the new democratic South Africa, first as Minister of Water-supply and -distribution, then as Minister of Education, child's play, a piece of cake.

Years later she began to approach and talk with me, in her well-spoken, educated, English accent, mostly about those people and groups who were persecuting her, chief among them whom were the SAS who had secretly infiltrated Ireland; also about the Eastern Health Board who were making problems for her, as were neighbours, she claimed.

Then, a revelation: she arrived in mufti, and unhooded. Her looks were quite Mediterranean or Near-Eastern, and she could well have been strikingly fine-looking when younger. From Kent, she'd once had a fiancé called M------ – "but I don't want to talk about him just now".

She could have stepped out of the atmospheric, sparse, desperate but marvellously-rendered Novellas of Jean Rhys.

(Song, most likely to sing:
   "They are hanging men and women
   For the wearing of the green.")

Ireland's answer to Bibendum, 'The Michelin Man'

AFTER all, the pneumatic tyre was invented and patented by John Boyd Dunlop, who then started the world's first factory in Stephen Street, Dublin, all in 1889.

For two or three years this man sauntered along his Parnell Street – Moore Street beat, sometimes with a spare can stuffed into each pocket of his track-suit trousers. I was perplexed by the leather straps criss-crossing his chest as if supporting a back-pack. Did he fear that if he took this harness off, he would fall apart, his "body burst open", like monster Grendel's in *Beowulf*? (When conducting an orchestra, Tchaikovsky, who felt himself to be permanently damned to 'Outer Darkness', would hold his head with one hand, fearing that otherwise it would fall off.)

In all fairness, the swastika was temporary. Later, also briefly, he sported a distinguished, neatly-trimmed beard.

One fine morning, as he moved forward, he was humming quietly, and dancing almost imperceptibly, grooving to his own music-scene: the hippest Dude in Town.

On several arctic nights one winter, when I was homeward bound, I spotted him slumped on the icy pavement half out of the same doorway: the first time, I 'phoned the local Gardai about his risk of exposure; I was warned that they knew him, that they'd investigate, and that I was not to approach!

Several months later, in early summer, he died suddenly of a heart attack, his slow, public, suicide over.

That little girl? I'm wondering if she'll one day take over my duties; and has already started her research – incognito.

Accordionist

AS HE played airs on his squeeze-box, always near O'Connell Bridge, this accordionist would sway slightly in time to the music, his face turning and even grimacing with concentration, his sightless eyes rolling so the irises disappeared, a quite disturbing thing to witness for young people.

Ireland has a long tradition of blind musicians, the most famous being harpist/composer Turlough O'Carolan (1670-1738) and Dublin's 'Zozimus' (Michael Moran, 1794-1846) who sang ballads in the streets.

These of course have their best-known counterparts among Afro-Americans in the USA during the twentieth century, most of them likewise from an impoverished class: Art Tatum, Sonny Terry, Ray Charles, Snooks Eaglin, Roland Kirk, Clarence Carter, Stevie Wonder and Reverend Gary Davis; Blind Lemon Jefferson, Blind Willie McTell, Blind Willie Johnson, Blind Boy Fuller, The Blind Boys of Alabama, and Blind Blake.

Humorists occasionally invent fictional Bluesmen, naming them 'Blind So-and-so'. They probably don't know that the visual impairment of those now-acclaimed musicians might have been avoided in childhood by early treatment at minimal cost, which they, and millions of their fellows, simply could not afford.

But a Blues song they were least likely to sing:
> *"Well, it wasn't no shack where I woke this mornin';*
> *I'd bin 'buked and scorned, but: No more scornin'!*
> *I didn't even owe no rent;*
> *I was now America's President!"*
> - from 'White House Holler', 2009

I particularly recommend the amplified version of this, with its grainy Bo Diddley-esque groove that has the youngsters at shriek-pitch excitement.

Bonus Blues!

> *"I've got a black-cat bone"??*
> *– Well, I have more!*
> *(Yer average puss has*
> *2 – 4 – 4).*
> *We're blessed with "floating"*
> *Collar-bones:*
> *So, gaps ? – no prob!*
> *No 'Sad Cat Moan'.*

From *Feelin' Feline Blues* (by Furry Lewis?)

End of Blues Interlude:

now it's back to the Liffey Delta…

Night, and I travelling

"Night, and I travelling…
I pass on into the darkness."
– Joseph Campbell

Graffiti Writer

FOR about four years in the late 1960s / early '70s extraordinary, cryptic slogans and statements appeared on walls and road signs during nights, anywhere along the seven miles between Dublin and Dun Laoghaire, striking the beholder with their cracked rhetoric. A smörgåsbord of splintered themes recurred: A bleak Irish-Catholic version of Christianity; 20th century history and politics; archetypal-ish myths; persecution (sometimes of a certain 'Lee' – does this name give us a clue as to the writer's identity?).

The bold, educated handwriting had a manic élan, wild yet controlled; it suggested that, walking in the small hours, the perpetrator scrawled his preoccupation of that moment speedily and succinctly on the nearest vertical surface, using chalks or wax-crayons of three or four colours.

Did 'FF' refer to the Government of that period, and why was there a circle around those letters, logo-like?

Hippie-era folkies 'Dr Strangely Strange' commemorated this mural Poète-manqué by incorporating some of his lines into a fine song 'Mary Malone of Moscow' on their second LP (1970).

Previously they had taken a distinguished friend, Robin Williamson of the magical, Scottish 'Incredible String Band' for a stroll around Dublin back-streets to show him the baffling messages, and he was so impressed that he wanted to name the forthcoming ISB album 'Who burns wonderful man to death?' Alas, powers-that-be vetoed such far-outness, and the record was released as 'Changing Horses' in 1969.

Who was this elusive author? What did his scribblings mean or refer to? Was any paranoia justified? Was there 'Reason in madness'? Or must one accept it as another mystery in the great scheme of things, 'Let the Mystery be'?

As Williamson had sung:
>*"If you answer this riddle…*
>*You'll never begin!"*

(I am grateful to Tim Booth of the aforementioned 'Strangelies' Trio for some of the information above. Tim Goulding wrote the graffiti-quoting song. Ivan Pawle was guest-pianist on 'Changing Horses').

National Stadium

National Stadium

" This year's
Guitar-Wizard! "
— N.M.E.

Who burns wonderful man to death?
—40 Morris-nurses
burnt every day in U.S.S.R.

Jews may tax
the North Pole

Lee, King
of
Kings!

 S.S.

The Ringsend Scavenger
(an imagined portrait)

ALAS, I did not encounter this gentleman, who several people have told me about. He operated in a locality I rarely frequented, trundling his bike through Sandymount and Donnybrook, even venturing into smart Merrion Square, gradually loading and draping his bike with scrap, the tyreless wheels surely emitting a terrible rattle, clatter or clanking.

He was dwelling in a primitive shack at the edge of Ringsend Dump (near the mouth of the river Liffey). A friend of mine considerately visited with a small supply of food not long before her wedding, but surprised him outside his door in the summer sunshine, bare-chested as he washed himself from a bowl of water: it seems he lived there uncontaminated by Dublin's rubbish or any noisome stink, almost a modern equivalent of those uncorruptible Celtic Saints and Hermits to whom young brides-to-be might make a devotional visitation and offering, receiving a holy blessing in return.

Liffey Boardwalk

I'D INTENDED to not draw any more bearded wanderers, but the man on the right was unsurpassed in one respect:

The narrator in Flann O'Brien's *At Swim-Two-Birds* recommends that authors should 'sample' (lift passages from) previous books, rather than bother to re-articulate well-known situations, feelings, etc. Consequently, I hope that the 'O'Brien' (Brian O'Nolan) estate will not be aggrieved if I borrow a phrase from *At Swim* which comments upon one Luke McFadden (the travelling tinsmith and masterly fiddler) and which also pertains to my little portrait:
'The smell of his clothes would knock you down.'

Most memorably, I was in a city centre Oxfam charity shop when he entered. Like in a pre-1940s H. M. Bateman cartoon, other browsers and customers rushed out. Trapped at the back, I staggered into a sorting room, gasping agitatedly to the startled manager, but too aghast to describe precisely the ammoniac stench and its intensity.

He was always serenely unaware of his affect on others. Impressively so!

The old gentleman in the middle seemed ancient and fragile, from a distant era, as if recently delivered from some institution after decades of incarceration: like a peripheral, quaint character in an early Tintin book, for instance *The Broken Ear* of 1937.

And who is the fellow on the left?
> *He comes,*
> *He goes,*
> *But no-one*
> *Knows!*

Bus-ridin' Man

THIS little senior citizen availed of his Free-Travel Pass by spending his days – and years – well wrapped up in a clean raincoat, riding on buses. Head bowed, he was ignored, and never spoke to anyone.

If I boarded a bus, for instance to Enniskerry, he'd dart a look at me, perhaps of recognition or curiosity, but a bit cowed, even wounded, as if beseeching some response. Hunched and unmoving, he stared into space, or at the beautiful Wicklow foothills. This daily travelling, for years, must have been soothing, timeless, preparing him maybe for his inevitable final journey:

> *For then, I, undistrest*
> *By hearts grown cold to me,*
> *Could lonely wait my endless rest*
> *With equanimity.*
> - Thomas Hardy

Those imploring glances may have achieved something. I hope he has now attained immortality. The last shall be first!

Walkabout (Australian Old-timer)

STRANGER in a strange land – Ireland – a primitive world where nature and civilisation collide with particular Irish failings: devious opportunism, money-siphoning, cute-hoor sleeveenery, a deluded sense of entitlement …

Thanks to such murky cunning, the marginalised become more so, the gap widens between them and the grasping 'haves' who became brazen during the 'Celtic Tigger' economic bubble, which then mutated into a runaway train:

> *Was it for this the wild geese spread*
> *The grey wing upon every tide;*
> *for this that all that blood was shed,*
> *For this Edward Fitzgerald died?*
> - from *September 1913* by W. B. Yeats

Unlike in 'The Railway Children' film, there was no resourceful Jenny Agutter heroine who, with her two siblings, flagged down the train, averting a disastrous crash. But here, someone shouting 'STOP!' would've been derided, even barged aside …

When will we ever learn?!!

A bad moment in recent Irish history.

Songwriter

In Kildare Street

Sequel: Poor Me!

A PORTRAIT of the Artist as prematurely
agèd, with Tundish*

*"We are all in the gutter, but some of us are looking at
the stars."* - Oscar Wilde

* "What funnel? – asked Stephen.
– The funnel through which you pour the oil into
your lamp. –
That? – said Stephen. Is that called a funnel? Is it
not a tundish? –
– What is a tundish? –
– That …the funnel. –
– Is that called a tundish in Ireland? asked the
dean. I never heard the word in my life. –
– It is called a tundish in Lower Drumcondra,
– said Stephen, laughing, – where they speak the
best English. –"
- from *A Portrait of the Artist as a Young Man,*
by James Joyce.

"Tragedy is undeveloped comedy."
- Patrick Kavanagh. DISCUSS!

And remember: Enjoy alcohol responsibly!
(Only drink a specific number of units each week,
as Jesus did).

Essay

by Patrick Pye

I WAS very happy when Rory Campbell asked me to write about his series of drawings of the eccentrics and stray folk who have, willy-nilly, accompanied us Dubliners (if sometimes only on the periphery of our vision) over the last sixty years. From the re-creation in coloured crayon of 'Toffee', the friend of his father – towering over the fledgling artist at the front door with chewy sweet in hand –to 'Michelin Man', bouncing along with his can, I have been privileged to witness the gestation of a world on the edge, fraught, comical, but never quite bereft of tenderness.

The appetite of our hunger for art begins with our need for self-expression. The intellectual hunger usually manifests itself more slowly with the appetite of curiosity. I suspect that in Rory it is the second appetite that has supplied the motive-force for these drawings. How do people who live on the street like this function? What forces them to reject the normality that we more ordinary folk fall into so more or less comfortably? In conversations with Rory over the last ten years there has been a recurring leitmotif concerning the celebration of the vigour of the street people. That, for the artist, is what these drawings are about.

It has to be acknowledged that the artist has made an unusual choice. What about the 'vigour' of sportsmen or climbers?

But behold! As with the would-be artist marking out himself, so with the layman: anhy man, or woman for that matter. Everything begins with self and its wonders and hurts; but so often in our wounds the hurt leaves us speechless, without the words or forms that would help us to cope, to know ourselves. We just may indeed end up with God, or Nature, or some crafty empowerment, but in the world of retired bank-managers the soul would appear to be deprived of the 'recognition' granted by the arts, the liberating word or form. It is such 'recognition' that gives the soul the dialogue, such room within itself, that frees it to face community with all its alarming variety.

Oft has it been remarked how close genius and madness lie to one another. Sometimes this becomes noticeable in the strife and storms of adolescence where the pressure of the 'other' bears down on the self. The strategy of adolescence is to avoid making the crossing for as long as we can … until language or some other moment of recognition grants an amelioration, a softening in the holed-up self. A good 94-year-old friend tells me in her wisdom that she has no notion how young people ride through adolescence, ending up normal and able to cope. How sweet then must be the multitudinous forms and possibilities provided in the arts where the eye covers the 'other' with a suddenly recognised seeing: where he is seen in the terms recognised by the see-er. Then the self may lose its hard solitude and commence its journey to a 'common humanity'.

Madness is a retreat. Maybe, more often than we suppose, it is a selected way out. Maybe all our oddnesses are willed and owned by ourselves, if we could but see.

I suspect that for Rory this publication represents his first venture before the Irish public. What an odd subject, you may exclaim, for such a venture! What an odd way to treat such a theme as the odd of this world, in a cartoon style, a style almost precious in its detail, yet dreamlike in the clarity of its colour-relations! How odd to make common crayon the medium for such a personal and distinct vision! How strange to use the remoteness of stylisation for such revelatory drawing!

But then, inadvertently and unselfconsciously, Rory is an original. And then, these images work. The solitude of his characters is immaculate and unbroken. Rory has been drawing in this cool and cerebral style for some twenty-five years but never to such effect. From the first drawing where the wanderer whom his father occasionally befriended, 'Toffee', fills the doorframe, I sense the wonder of the incipient artist before the mighty visitor holding out his imminent hand with the offer of scarlet pleasure. It is a surreal image but totally convincing of the child's experience of the Stranger, like a prophet who has suddenly alighted from Mars. The eerie colour is evocative of all that distance between the planets, and the uncanny clarity translates the scent of youthful experience for greater maturity. Even the ambivalence of the scarlet sweet heightens the strangeness of the encounter.

Again and again the impersonality of the line and the understatement of the image play into the lunatic unexpectedness of what is actually happening in the street. Whether it is the 'Solo Dancer of the Pillar', reflected ingenuously for our generation in the glossy metal of the Spire, or the well-known haunter of bookshops in 'Food, and for thought', the loneliness here described is exact and tart, and seen with remarkable poetry and kindliness.

Rory Campbell has had the benign idea of celebrating those souls among us whom we often confine to the periphery of our vision, and he has done this in a telling and inimitable manner that no one would have guessed at.
May I introduce you to the Master of the Common Crayon …

Patrick Pye, RHA
Tallaght

Introduction to
Gerard Brady's Photographs

I WAS completing my own series of portraits when I was introduced by the Rowan family in Booterstown to Gerard Brady in order to see photographs he made from 1970 to 1975, hitherto unseen by the public, of unusual Dublin denizens. I was struck by how our pictures shared certain qualities – and complemented each other – having sprung from a similar interest.

Gerard Brady (1929-2010) grew up in the Dorset Street area of the North Inner City, a fourth-generation Dubliner. His father sold second-hand books near the river Liffey, and Gerard did this as a sideline while also working as a Civil Servant for twenty years. He then founded a successful business in the specialist field of law searching, subsequently qualifying and occasionally practising as a Barrister.

From the mid-1940s on, with a state-of-the-art camera brought back from post-war Europe, he began to take photographs seriously (for instance, of Dublin street life), also using his own photos to illustrate articles he wrote on Travel and History for 'Independent' newspapers. In 1957 his biography of Saint Dominic titled, 'Saint Dominic, Pilgrim of Light', containing his recent black-and-white images of France, Spain and Italy, was published in London and New York.

For years, walking through Dublin during his working day, he would notice the same extraordinary 'characters', but only began to snap them covertly in 1970 when he had fixed a specialised lens to his Zeiss Contaflex camera. This 'Angle-finder' lens, normally used in scientific and medical laboratories, enabled him to shoot at a 90-degree angle, i.e. to photograph a person or people to one or another side of him when he was looking and pointing the camera straight ahead. Brady's subjects were unconscious that the man pottering nearby and snapping away harmlessly was, in fact, capturing images of them at their most typical – almost like a quick-witted spy, clandestine yet with appreciation and respect, usually operating on the spur of the moment as someone eminently suitable hove into view.

His contemporary, French nanny Vivian Maier (1926-2009), who likewise snapped street life (of New York and Chicago) in many superb photographs, occasionally informed people that she was 'a spy'!

By 1975 Gerard felt he had completed this particular series; thus it represents a half-decade from more than forty years ago, when his camera saved these citizens from obscurity or oblivion, by recording them for posterity: an unflinching, thought-provoking, evocative and visually striking time-and-place capsule.

Rory Campbell
2014

Not untypical habitat: Brabazon Row. Etching by James McCreary.

Just over 300 years earlier, in 1667, Jonathan Swift was born feet away from here, in Hoey's Court (long demolished).

Not Downing Street

With his cigarette and gritty gaze, this could be a French 'Penseur' or film actor.

We have a rare sighting here of the striped, woven carrier-bag, with orange nylon handles, immensely strong and 'environmental', made, I think, by Irish Ropes in Newbridge, County Kildare, which were ubiquitous then.

Busker...

… a few years later.

Al fresco – one of the great interpreters of Samuel Beckett? But just which play is it?
The battered oil–drum must be a clue.

(In the decade that taste forgot) "Après le déluge, moi!"

"The lowest and most dejected thing of fortune? Unaccomodated man is no more but such a poor, bare, forked animal as thou art." – Shakespeare, 'King Lear'.

Yet, a fine sculpture could be made out of this figure. (Please excuse any sententiousness!)

Acknowledgements

Photograph: Mel Cameron

I MUST especially thank specific people, including friends and artists, for their invaluable practical help and encouragement while I worked on this project:

Gerard brady, then his widow Ann, and their son Paul, for allowing me to showcase his unique photographs so gladly; Mel Cameron for her photos of Tamasin-behind-pumpkin, and of me; Tom Campbell for his financial acumen; Doreen Grogan and Grahame Spencer at 'Aungier Print' for their expert assistance with the black-and-white photocopying; James and Thérèse Gorry for permission to reproduce the painting of Killiney Bay; Peter Hanan who gave me 'Polychromos' pencils of many colours, and scanned Gerard Brady's photographs; Seán Hillen for recommending a superior colour-photocopy paper,

and for scanning work-in-progress; (in Dorset)
Stanislaw Lenartowicz, and Venessa Shearwood who
gave me locally-made drawing-books, then crucial
feedback and support from start to finish; James
McCreary for allowing me to reproduce his exquisite
etching 'Brabazon Row'; Nick Maxwell for some ideas
on book-design; the late Edward Murphy, visionary
Chief Librarian at the National College of Art and
Design for more than 30 years; Peter Murray for his
detailed account of a fascinating recluse in South
County Dublin (on the edge of Bray); Paula Nolan for
her expertise, imagination and dedication in designing
this book; James and Taffina O'Nolan for reminding
me of conspicuous people worth portraying; David
Pearson and John Wyse-Jackson, my University
contemporaries, for keeping me on my toes; Nóirín and
Patrick Pye (who wrote his meditative
piece with a will), and Hilary Pyle
for her perceptive preface (also
for valuing my powers of
memory!): I could not wish
for more insightful essays.

Thanks also to Seán and Gary
O'Reilly, and staff, at 'Reads Photocopiers'
in Nassau Street; to Stephen Stokes for
shrewd advice and tips on marketing my
project; Pat Taylor for consistent kindness
and helpfulness over decades; Damien
White, whose skilled practical wizardry
solved and fixed problems and emergencies
in house and garden, even at short notice,
over years; and my goodly neighbours 'ere:
Andrew and Attracta Manson, Rosemary Ryan, Pat
Reynolds, Rosa Seta, Cliona Murphy, and Esmé from
Rotterdam.

Finally, to Pansy and Tamasin, perennially affectionate,
often infuriating, since more than 16 years ago, and
for their miraculously clean paws when unexpectedly
jumping onto, slumping down on, or rolling over a
picture I'm working on … oops!

And Pablo, their Blues-mewin' neighbour, for being
endearingly magnificent.

Photograph: Mel Cameron

Biography

Rory Campbell was born in 1951, and grew up, the third of five brothers, near Shanganagh (pronounced: Shan-ganna) bridge in South County Dublin. His parents were 'Anglo-Irish', but on his father's side there was also a tradition of romantic and risky struggle for Irish Independence, since the United Irishmen of the 1790s, and well into the 20th century.

After schools in the locality, then Sussex when a teenager (where his mother had been raised), he studied English at Trinity College, Dublin.

Among other very interesting jobs, Rory has drawn cartoon, illustrations and graphic-design images for publications and official organisations here and abroad; and has also occasionally contributed articles or written material on popular culture to national and international journals.

He has received several Aer Lingus/Arts Council Travel Awards, enabling him to investigate visual culture and traditions in France, England and Italy.

In 2013 he exhibited paintings in Ireland, and the UK in 2014. Currently he is working on another series of portraits, this time of fascinating women, entitled 'Eclectic Ladyland'.

(Since he was about 10, Rory has fantasised about drumming in a great band, but done nothing about it except listen to, and see, excellent drummers and musicians).

He lives in the beautiful county of Wicklow.

A Note on My Working-Method

MOST of the pictures in this book were made in the same way: I begin by sketching the portraits with a soft pencil on A4-size cartridge paper, then with hollow-nibbed technical-pens draw, in black ink, over the sketch. Having rubbed out all the pencil lines, I correct and improve the drawing with black and white inks.

Next, I photocopy the drawing onto creamy colour-photography paper, then, finally, colour that, improvising all the while. For heads, hands and small details, I use Faber-Castell 'Polychromos' colour-pencils; for most clothing and backgrounds, I use 'Caran d'Ache Neocolor-2' (water-soluble) crayons. Occasionally on a small area I use vivid inks.